My Stories Abo

WRITTEN BY
SARAH FLETCHER

ART BY
DON KUEKER

Publishing House
St. Louis London

Unless otherwise stated, all Bible quotations used in this book are from the Revised
Standard Version, copyright 1946 and 1952 by the Division of Christian Education of
the National Council of the Churches of Christ in the United States of America, or
from Today's English Version, copyright by the American Bible Society, 1966.

Concordia Publishing House, St. Louis, Missouri
Concordia Publishing House Ltd., London, E. C. 1
Copyright © 1974 Concordia Publishing House
ISBN 0-570-03427-2

MANUFACTURED IN THE UNITED STATES OF AMERICA

The First Christmas

One day an angel came to a young girl called Mary and told her that she was going to have a baby. The baby would be God's Son, Jesus. Mary got married to a good man called Joseph. They were very happy.

"I wish we could live right here in our home town, Mary," said Joseph, "because you are going to have your baby very soon. But the king wants to count his people, and we have to go all the way to Bethlehem to be counted."

"That's all right, Joseph," said Mary. "God will take care of us."

It took a long time to get to Bethlehem back then because there weren't any cars or trains or airplanes. People had to walk or ride on little donkeys. But finally Joseph and Mary got there. It was nighttime, and they were very tired. And do you know what? They couldn't find anywhere to stay! All the hotels were full.

"We just have to find somewhere to stay!" Joseph told one hotel man. "My wife is going to have her baby very soon!"

"Well," said the hotel man, "I guess you can stay in my stable with the animals if you want to."

"Oh, thank you!" said Joseph. He and Mary hurried to the stable. Soon a little baby was born there—Jesus. And a big beautiful star appeared in the sky and hung right over the stable where Jesus was born.

To us a child is born.

Isaiah 9:6

The Shepherds

Outside Bethlehem were some hills, and on these hills were shepherds taking care of their sheep. It was late at night and most of the shepherds had wrapped themselves up in their big, fuzzy cloaks to keep warm.

Suddenly an angel came and the whole sky was full of light. The shepherds were afraid, but the angel said: "Don't be afraid! I have good news for you. God's own Son, Jesus, has been born tonight in Bethlehem." Then many more angels came and they all sang "Glory to God!"

After the angels went back to heaven, the shepherds decided to hurry right down to Bethlehem and see Baby Jesus for themselves. Off they went to the stable.

"What a wonderful baby!" they said to Mary and Joseph. Then they told lots of other people about Jesus and everybody was happy.

Glory to God!

Luke 2:14

The Wise Men

Far, far away from Bethelem lived some wise men. They knew about the stars and a great many other things. But one night they saw a star that they had never seen before. It shone very brightly.

"What is this new star?" they asked. "We'd better look it up in some of our books."

In one of the books they read that the bright star had come to show them where their Savior, God's Son, was born. So they decided to get on their camels and go see Baby Jesus.

For miles and miles and miles they rode, bouncing and swaying on the bumpy camels. And at last, after a very long time, they came to Bethlehem and the house where Mary and Joseph lived.

"We would like to see the baby," they said. "We have traveled a long way."

"All right," said Mary and Joseph. "Please come in."

When the wise men saw Baby Jesus, they kneeled down in front of Him. Then they gave Him some wonderful presents. Mary was glad that they loved Jesus so much.

We have come to worship Him.

Matthew 2:2

Jesus in the Temple

When Jesus was 12 years old, Mary and Joseph decided to take Him to the big church in Jerusalem for a special celebration. Many people came to the celebration, and Jesus saw His uncles and aunts and cousins and friends there.

After the celebration, everybody went home again — everybody except Jesus. Mary and Joseph *thought* He was with His cousins and friends. But He wasn't.

"Oh, dear!" said Mary. "Where is Jesus?"

"We shall have to go back to Jerusalem and look for Him," said Joseph.

After a long time Mary and Joseph found Jesus in the big church. He was talking to the teachers.

"Why did You get lost, Jesus?" asked Mary.

"I wasn't lost, Mother," said Jesus. "I was talking to these teachers about My Father in heaven."

"Well, let's go home now," said Joseph. And they did.

I keep God's teaching
in my heart.

Psalm 40:8, *para.*

Jesus and John

After Jesus grew up, He went on a long trip.

The first place He went was to the Jordan River. There He met His cousin, John the Baptizer. John had been telling people that Jesus was coming.

"Hello, John!" said Jesus. "I would like you to baptize Me."

John's eyes got big. "Oh, I couldn't do *that,* Jesus," he said. "I am only a man, and You are the Son of God."

"That's all right, John," said Jesus. "God *wants* you to baptize Me."

So Jesus and John walked into the water and John baptized Jesus. Then a wonderful thing happened. A beautiful dove flew down from the sky and floated by Jesus' head. And the voice of God spoke.

"This is My own dear Son," said God, "and I am very happy with Him."

"I baptize you with water," said John,
"but Jesus will baptize you with God's Spirit."

Matthew 3:11, *para.*

Jesus and the Sick People

Jesus didn't like people to be sick. So when sick people came to see Him, He made them well again. He made blind people able to see. He made crippled people able to walk. He made people with terrible diseases and big sores healthy.

One time a man came to Jesus and said, "Jesus, my little girl is very sick. Please help her."

"All right," said Jesus. But on the way to the man's house they met some other men who said, "You're too late, Jesus. The little girl is dead."

"No, she isn't," said Jesus. "She's just asleep." He came to the man's house and went into the little girl's room. "Wake up, little girl!" He said.

The little girl woke up. She was well!

Many people heard about the wonderful things Jesus was doing. Everywhere He went they brought more sick people to see Him. And Jesus made them all well again.

Praise the Lord!
He heals all my diseases.

Psalm 103:2, 3

Jesus and the Children

Have you ever wanted to see something very much — like a parade or a show or just something happening on your street — and you couldn't see it because there were too many people in front of you? Didn't that make you sad and just a little bit angry because you were so small?

Well, sometimes the same thing happened to children in Bible times. They wanted to see Jesus as much as the grown-ups did, but the grown-ups got in the way.

One day some mothers took their little children through the crowd and right up to where Jesus was.

"Stop that!" said some of Jesus' helpers to the mothers. "Don't bother Jesus with these children."

"No," said Jesus. "Don't stop the mothers. I *want* to see the children. God loves children very much."

And Jesus hugged the children and talked to them and played with them.

Jesus said,
"Let the children come to Me."

Matthew 19:14

Jesus and the Storm

One day Jesus and His helpers got into a boat to go to the other side of a big lake. Jesus had been working hard, and He was very tired. So He went to sleep.

While He was sleeping, a big storm blew up. KKK-THUD! went the thunder. CRAAACK! went the lightning. SWOOSH! went the wind. And SPLOSH! SPLOSH! went the big waves against the side of the boat. SPLOSH! SPLOSH! SPLOSH! Soon the waves got *inside* the boat and it started to sink.

"Jesus! Wake up!" cried His helpers. They were so scared they could hardly move. "Jesus!" they cried. "We're going to die!"

Jesus got up. "Be quiet, wind!" He ordered. "Be quiet, water!" And they were. The whole lake was as quiet as if there had never been a storm at all.

"What a wonderful man Jesus is!" said all His helpers.

Our God is a God who saves.

Psalm 68:20

Jesus Tells a Story

One time a bunch of people whom nobody liked very much came to listen to Jesus tell about God's love. Some other people who thought *they* were pretty special got angry.

"Why do you talk to these people nobody else likes?" they asked Jesus. Instead of just answering them, Jesus told them a story.

"Once upon a time," said Jesus, "there was a shepherd who had a hundred sheep. Ninety-nine of these sheep were good and never gave the shepherd any trouble. But one little sheep was bad. He was always getting into trouble.

"One day the bad little sheep decided to take a walk all by himself. He *knew* the shepherd didn't want him to. He *knew* the shepherd was afraid a bear or a wolf might eat a little sheep walking by himself. But that bad little sheep did it anyway. And sure enough, he got lost.

"When the shepherd saw that his bad little sheep was gone, he began to worry.

" 'You stay here,' he said to the other sheep, and he went off to look for the lost one.

"He looked and looked and finally he found that bad little sheep and took him home again. And then the shepherd and the bad little sheep and all the other sheep were very happy.

"These people that nobody likes are like that bad little sheep," said Jesus. "They need to know that God loves them."

Rejoice with me,
for I have found my lost sheep!

Luke 15:6

19

Jesus Comes to Jerusalem

Bzzzz! "Is He coming?" "I think I see Him!" "No, not yet."

People, people, and more people lined up along the Jerusalem street. Many of them held palm branches that looked like bright green banners. Children bounced up and down like rubber balls. Everyone was so excited. Jesus was coming to Jerusalem!

"Here He comes!" cried a little girl, pointing and waving.

And sure enough! Along the street came Jesus, riding on a little donkey. His helpers were with Him.

"Hosanna, Lord!" shouted the people. "Glory to God!"

But a few crabby men grumbled. "Make these people be quiet, Jesus."

"No," said Jesus. "I am happy that the people are shouting and praising, and so is My Father in heaven. He has sent Me to you so you can be His friends always. This is a wonderful day!"

God bless Him
who comes in the name of the Lord!

Mark 11:9

Jesus Prays

Jesus knew that God, His Father, had some important work for Him to do. Bad things would happen to Jesus while He was doing this work—things that hurt. Jesus knew that too, but He also knew that He had to be hurt so people could be God's friends forever.

One evening Jesus decided to talk to God about the work He had to do. He decided to go to a garden just outside Jerusalem to pray. And He asked some of His helpers to go with Him and keep Him company. When they got to the garden, Jesus kneeled down.

"O holy Father," He prayed, "please be with Me and with My people. I will do whatever You want Me to, Father."

When Jesus finished praying, He looked at His helpers. They had all gone to sleep. They hadn't even stayed awake to keep Him company. Jesus felt very sad.

I will do whatever
You want me to, God.

Luke 22:42, *para.*

Jesus Is Arrested

While Jesus was still in the garden, some soldiers came to arrest Him. They tied His hands, and Jesus didn't even try to stop them. Jesus' helpers got scared and ran away. Now Jesus was all alone with the people who hated Him.

First the soldiers took Jesus to see a group of men called the Council.

"Are You God's Son?" the Council asked Jesus.

"Yes, I am," said Jesus.

"You are a bad Person!" said the Council.

Then they spit on Jesus and beat Him. It hurt Jesus very much.

Next the soldiers took Jesus to see Pilate, the Roman governor. Pilate asked Jesus a lot of questions, and then he said, "I don't think Jesus has done anything wrong. But you can do whatever you want with Him."

And so the bad people decided to kill Jesus.

He was hurt
because of the bad things we do.

Isaiah 53:5, *para.*

Jesus Dies

The bad people took Jesus to a rocky hill outside Jerusalem. They made Him carry a heavy wooden cross. Poor Jesus was so tired and hurt that He kept falling down. Finally a nice man called Simon carried the cross for Him.

When they got to the top of the hill, the bad people nailed Jesus' hands and feet to the cross. Then they stuck the cross in the ground and left Jesus there to die.

Jesus hung on the cross for a long time. People shouted mean things at Him, and He hurt very much. But all the time Jesus knew that He was doing what God wanted Him to. He knew that because of what He was doing, all the people in the world could be God's friends forever.

Jesus even prayed for the bad people who had hurt Him. "Forgive them, Father," He said. "They don't know what they are doing."

And at last Jesus died and the whole earth turned dark.

Jesus gave His life for us.

1 John 3:16, *para.*

Jesus Is Alive!

After Jesus died, some of His friends took His body off the cross and put it in a cave on the side of a hill. The soldiers rolled a big rock in front of the cave and stood by it day and night. They didn't want anybody to steal Jesus' body.

Early one morning two days after Jesus died, some very brave women went to the cave. They were going to ask the soldiers if they could put perfume on Jesus' body.

The women just got to the cave when the earth began to shake. A beautiful angel appeared and rolled the big rock away. The soldiers were so frightened that they couldn't move.

"Don't be afraid," the angel told the women. "Jesus isn't here anymore. He's alive! Now run and tell everyone."

Off ran the women and on their way guess who they met? Jesus! They were really happy then and ran around telling everybody, "Jesus is alive!"

He has risen!

Matthew 28:6

Jesus Goes to Heaven

For forty days after Jesus came alive again, He went around visiting His helpers. They were all so happy to see Him!

But then Jesus knew that His work was done. It was time for Him to go back to heaven and be with God. Of course He would still be with all the people on earth too. He can be everywhere at the same time because He is the Son of God. But people wouldn't be able to see Him on earth anymore.

So one day Jesus went with His helpers to a place called Bethany. He raised His hands and blessed them, and then He began to rise toward heaven. After a while a cloud covered Jesus, and His helpers couldn't see Him anymore. But they knew they'd see Jesus again when *they* went to heaven—just as we will.

Jesus said,
"I will be with you always."

Matthew 28:20